BUDGET PLANNER FOR BEGINNER:

Navigating Your Finances with Confidence and Ease.

BUDGET PLANNER

for beginners

COPYRIGHT © 2023 BY MIKE PETERSON

This book is designed to provide accurate and authoritative information regarding the subject matter covered. It is sold with the understanding that the publisher is not engaged in rendering legal, accounting, or other professional services. If legal advice or other professional assistance is required, the services of a competent professional should be

sought.

ABOUT THE AUTHOR

Mike Peterson is a certified financial and portfolio management personnel , dedicated to empowering individuals in their financial journeys. With a passion for simplifying complex financial concepts, Mike Peterson strives to make budgeting and financial management accessible to beginners.

As a seasoned financial] professional, Mike Peterson brings a wealth of experience to the table. Beyond the pages of this book, he actively engages in relevant activities, such as writing for financial publications, hosting workshops, etc.

PURPOSE OF THE BOOK

This book is your key to financial empowerment. Its purpose is to demystify budgeting, making

it is accessible and actionable for beginners. By providing a clear roadmap, it aims to instill confidence in your financial decisions, setting you on a path to lasting financial well-being.

Overview of the Importance of Budgeting:

Budgeting is the cornerstone of financial success. It's not just about tracking expenses; it's a

strategic tool that aligns your spending with your goals. From gaining control over your money to building savings and investments, budgeting unlocks the doors to financial freedom.

WHAT READERS CAN EXPECT TO GAIN

Embark on a transformative financial journey as you delve into the pages of "Budget Planner for Beginners: Navigating Your Finances with Confidence and Ease." This comprehensive guide is meticulously crafted to equip readers with invaluable insights, practical strategies, and the confidence needed to take charge of their financial destinies. Here's a voluminous overview of what readers can expect to gain:

1. Mastery of Budgeting Essentials

- Insight: Gain a deep understanding of budgeting principles, making financial management clear, accessible, and empowering.

2. Building a Robust Budget

- Practical Guidance: Learn step-by-step how to create a personalized and effective budget tailored to your unique financial goals and llifestyle.

3. Strategic Savings Strategies

  - Actionable Tips: Unlock the secrets of successful saving, with actionable strategies to build emergency funds, achieve short-term goals, and secure your financial ffuture.

4. Investing Demystified

  - Foundational Knowledge: Grasp the basics of investing, understand different investment options, and learn how to make informed decisions to grow your wealth.

5. Debt Management Expertise

- Debt Reduction Tactics: Explore effective methods to manage and eliminate debt, allowing you to regain control of your financial freedom.

6. Smart Spending Habits

- Learn to differentiate between needs and wants, cultivating responsible spending habits for sustained financial health.

TABLE OF CONTENT

WELCOME AND PURPOSE OF THE BOOK

BRIEF OVERVIEW Of THE IMPORTANCE OF BUDGETING

WHAT READERS CAN EXPECT TO GAIN

CHAPTER 1: INTRODUCTION TO BUDGETING

1. Why Budgeting Matters

2. Benefits of Budgeting

3. Understanding Income and Expenses

4. Identifying Income Sources

5. Categorizing Expenses

CHAPTER 2: CREATING YOUR PERSONAL BUDGET

CHAPTER 3: SMART SPENDING HABITS

5. Insurance and Financial Security

CHAPTER 4: INVESTING BASICS FOR BEGINNERS

1. Introduction to Investments

2. Low-Risk Investment Options

3. Tracking and Adjusting Your Budget

4. Regular Budget Reviews

5. Adapting to Life Changes

CHAPTER 5: BUILDING A SUSTAINABLE FINANCIAL FUTURE

1. Long-Term Financial Planning

2. Retirement Savings

3. Pitfalls to Watch Out For

4. Learning from Mistakes

CHAPTER 6: SUCCESS STORIES AND TIPS FROM BUDGETING PRO

1. Success stories

2. Tips from budgeting **pros**

CONCLUSION

1. Recap of Key Takeaways

2. Encouragement for Continued Financial Growth

<u>INTRODUCTION</u>

Welcome to "Budget Planner for Beginners: Navigating Your Finances with Confidence and Ease." In a world filled with financial complexities, this book serves as your compass, guiding you through the fundamental principles of budgeting to empower you on your journey toward financial well-being. Understanding and managing your finances shouldn't be an intimidating task. Whether you're just starting your career, entering a new phase of life, or simply looking to take control of your money, this book is tailored to provide you with practical insights and actionable steps. In this introduction, we'll explore why budgeting matters, the benefits it can bring to your life,

and what you can expect to gain from the pages that follow. Consider this book your partner in building a solid foundation for your financial future.

Let's embark on this journey together, where

financial confidence and ease await you.

CHAPTER 1

INTRODUCTION TO BUDGETING

Budgeting isn't just about numbers; it's a powerful tool that puts you in control of your financial narrative. In this chapter, we explore why budgeting matters—how it transforms money from a source of stress into a vehicle for your dreams. Discover the benefits that extend beyond the balance sheet: clarity, empowerment, and the freedom to shape your financial future. Buckle up as we embark on a journey to demystify budgeting and pave the way for financial success.

WHY BUDGETING MATTERS

At its core, budgeting is the compass that directs your financial journey. It's not just about restricting spending; it's a strategic plan that empowers you to allocate your resources purposefully. Budgeting matters because it provides clarity, control, and a roadmap for achieving your financial aspirations. It transforms money from a source of stress into a tool for building the life you desire.

BENEFITS OF BUDGETING

1. Financial Clarity: Budgeting unveils a clear picture of where your money comes from and where it goes. It's a flashlight in the financial fog, illuminating your financial landscape.

2. Empowered Decision-Making: With a budget, you become the master of your financial destiny. You decide how to allocate funds based on your priorities, goals and value

3. Debt Management: Budgeting helps you tackle and eliminate debt strategically. It's a powerful tool for breaking free from financial burdens and building a debt-free future.

4. Savings and Investments: By budgeting, you cultivate the habit of saving. It's the foundation for creating an emergency fund, achieving short-term goals, and venturing into the world of investments.

5. Stress Reduction: Financial uncertainty can be stressful. Budgeting alleviates this stress by providing a structured plan, fostering financial confidence, and allowing you to weather unexpected financial storms.

In this chapter, we delve into the core reasons why budgeting is a fundamental skill for financial success. As you grasp the importance, you'll be better equipped to embark on your budgeting journey with purpose and enthusiasm.

UNDERSTANDING INCOME AND EXPENSES

Income and expenses are the financial heartbeat of your life, dictating the rhythm of your financial journey.

What is Income?

Income encompasses all the money flowing into your life. It's not just your salary; it includes

side hustles, bonuses, and any other source contributing to your financial pool. Understanding Your various income streams are the first step in harnessing their potential.

What are Expenses?

Expenses, on the other hand, represent the outflows—where your money goes. From bills to discretionary spending, expenses cover a spectrum of financial commitments. By dissecting and categorizing these expenditures, you gain a comprehensive view of your financial landscape.

In the intricate dance between income and expenses, we lay the foundation for effective budgeting. Join us as we explore the nuances of these financial elements, providing you with the insights needed to navigate your financial terrain with confidence.

In the financial realm, knowledge is power. To harness this power, we begin by unraveling the intricacies of your financial inflows and outflows. This chapter is your compass to navigating the seas of income and expenses, ensuring you have a clear map of your financial landscape.

IDENTIFYING INCOME SOURCES

Your financial journey starts with understanding where your money comes from. From salaries to side hustles, we explore the various streams that contribute to your income. Uncover the nuances of each source, empowering you to make informed decisions about your earning potential.

Categorizing Expenses

Just as important as knowing your income is understanding where it goes. In this subchapter, We delve into the art of categorizing expenses. From fixed bills to discretionary spending, gain insights into organizing your expenditures. This skill is the cornerstone of effective budgeting, providing the clarity needed to make intentional financial choices. As we navigate through the labyrinth of income and expenses, you'll emerge equipped with the knowledge to wield your financial resources strategically. Get ready to take charge of your financial destiny by mastering the fundamentals of income and expense management.

CHAPTER 2

<u>CREATING YOUR PERSONAL BUDGET</u>

Budgeting is your financial blueprint, and in this chapter, we embark on the journey of crafting a personalized plan tailored to your aspirations and lifestyle. Setting Your financial goals are the compass that guides your budgeting expedition. We delve into the art of setting goals that are not just wishful thinking but tangible, measurable targets. Whether it's building an emergency fund, paying off debt, or saving for a specific purpose, your goals become the driving force behind your budget.

Crafting Realistic Goals: We explore the importance of realism in goal-setting, ensuring your financial aspirations are achievable within your current circumstances.

Measuring Success: Learn how to create benchmarks and milestones to measure your progress, celebrating each financial victory along the way.

Allocating Budget Categories With goals in sight, it's time to bring structure to your financial landscape through careful category allocation.

Essential Categories: Dive into the core categories like housing, utilities, and groceries, understanding how to allocate funds to cover your **basic need Discretionary Spending:** Explore the world of discretionary spending, from entertainment to dining out. Discover the balance between enjoyment and financial responsibility.

Emergency Funds and Savings: Allocate a portion of your budget to emergency funds and savings, nurturing financial security and resilience. As we navigate the intricacies of goal-setting and category allocation, your budget transforms from a mere financial plan into a dynamic tool for achieving your dreams. Join us as we demystify the process, providing you with the insights and tools to create a budget that not only reflects your financial reality but also propels you toward a future of financial success.

SAVING STRATEGIES FOR BEGINNERS

Defining Saving

At its essence, saving is the deliberate act of setting aside money for future use rather than immediate consumption. It's a financial reservoir that provides a safety net, fuels your aspirations, and empowers you to navigate life's uncertainties.

Importance of Savings

- Safeguarding Financial Stability: Savings act as a buffer against unexpected expenses, offering a sense of financial security and stability.
- Opportunity Creation: Savings pave the way for seizing opportunities, whether it's

investing in education, starting a business, or embarking on a dream vacation.

- Debt Prevention and Reduction: A robust savings cushion prevents the need to rely on credit for unforeseen expenses, reducing the risk of falling into debt traps.

SAVING STRATEGIES

Saving is the act of setting aside a portion of your income for future use rather than spending it immediately. It involves creating a financial cushion to address unexpected expenses, work towards financial goals, and build a foundation for long-term financial security.

1. Start Small, Start Now: Begin with a modest amount you can comfortably set aside. Consistency

is key, and even small contributions add up over time.

2. Automate Your Savings: Set up automatic transfers to your savings account. This ensures that a portion of your income is saved before you have the chance to spend it.

3. Emergency Fund Priority: Allocate a portion of your savings to build an emergency fund. This fund serves as a financial lifeline during unexpected challenges.

4. Goal-Based Savings: Define specific savings goals, whether it's for a vacation, a down payment, or a rainy day fund. Having clear objectives enhances your motivation to save.

5. Cut Unnecessary Expenses: Identify areas in your discretionary spending where you can cut back. Redirect these funds toward your savings goals.

In this chapter, we unravel the importance of saving and equip you with practical strategies to kickstart your savings journey. Whether you're aiming for financial stability, opportunity creation, for debt reduction, the art of saving is a cornerstone of your path to financial success.

<u>DEBT MANAGEMENT</u>

Debt can be a powerful tool, but navigating its terrain requires strategic management. In this chapter, we unravel the intricacies of debt, exploring various types and providing actionable steps to master the art of debt management.

Types of Debt

- Secured Debt: Tied to assets like mortgages or car loans, secured debts involve collateral.
- Defaulting on payments may result in the loss of the asset.
- Unsecured Debt: Examples include credit card debt and medical bills. Without

collateral, these debts often carry higher interest rates.

- Good Debt vs. Bad Debt: Distinguish between debt incurred for appreciating assets (good debt) and debt for non-essential expenses (bad debt).

Creating a Debt Repayment Plan

1. Assess Your Debt: Compile a detailed list of your debts, including amounts owed, interest rates, and minimum payments.
2. Prioritize High-Interest Debt: Tackle debts with higher interest rates first to minimize overall
3. interest costs.

4. Snowball vs. Avalanche Method: Choose a strategy that suits your psychology—either paying off the smallest debts first (snowball) or focusing on the highest interest rate debts (avalanche).

5. Negotiate Terms: Reach out to creditors to explore options such as lower interest rates or modified repayment plans.

6. Create a Realistic Budget: Allocate a dedicated portion of your budget for debt repayment, ensuring consistency in your efforts.

7. Seek Professional Advice: Consider consulting with financial advisors or debt counselors for personalized guidance and support.

8. This chapter serves as your guide to mastering debt dynamics. Whether you're

aiming to eliminate high-interest debt, understanding the nuances of good and bad debt, or crafting a strategic repayment plan, you'll emerge equipped to navigate the complexities of debt and regain control of your financial journey

CHAPTER 3

<u>SMART SPENDING HABITS</u>

Smart spending is the cornerstone of financial health. In this chapter, we delve into the art of distinguishing between needs and wants and provide practical tips for cultivating responsible spending habits.

Differentiating Needs vs. Wants

Needs: Essential for survival and well-being, needs include basics like food, shelter, clothing, and healthcare.

Wants*:* Desirable but non-essential items, wants encompass luxury goods, entertainment, and other discretionary purchases.

Understanding this distinction forms the basis for making intentional spending decisions.

Tips For Responsible Spending

Create a Budget: A budget acts as your spending guide, helping you allocate funds to both needs and wants in a controlled manner.

- ***Prioritize Needs:*** Ensure your basic needs are met before allocating funds to discretionary spending. This ensures financial stability.

- ***Practice Delayed Gratification***: Before making non-essential purchases, give yourself time to evaluate their importance. Delaying gratification reduces impulse spending.

- ***Comparison Shopping:*** Research and compare prices before making purchases. This simple step can lead to significant savings.

- ***Set Spending Limits***: Establish limits for discretionary spending categories. This prevents overspending and encourages conscious choices.

- Emergency Fund: Maintain an emergency fund to cover unexpected expenses, reducing the likelihood of dipping into discretionary funds.

- ***Track and Review:*** Regularly review your spending habits. Tracking expenses provides insights into patterns and opportunities for improvement.

- ***Quality Over Quantity:*** Prioritize quality over quantity. Invest in items that offer long-term value rather than succumbing to the allure of cheap, short-lived purchases.

Mastering the art of smart spending empowers you to enjoy life's pleasures while maintaining financial stability. By differentiating between needs and wants and implementing responsible spending practices, you'll cultivate a healthy relationship with your finances, setting the stage for long-term financial success.

Emergency Funds and Financial Security

Financial security is not just about earning; it's about safeguarding what you've earned. This chapter focuses on the critical elements of building an emergency fund and understanding the role of insurance in achieving comprehensive financial security.

Purpose of an Emergency Fund

Understand that an emergency fund acts as a financial safety net, providing a cushion in times of unexpected expenses or income disruption.

- How Much to Save: Aim for three to six months' worth of living expenses in your emergency fund. This ensures you have sufficient coverage for various unexpected situations.

- Consistency in Contributions: Regularly contribute to your emergency fund, treating it as a non-negotiable expense in your budget.

- Accessible Yet Separate: Keep your emergency fund easily accessible, but separate from your daily spending accounts to avoid casual withdrawals.

- Rebuilding After Use: If you dip into your emergency fund, prioritize rebuilding it as soon as possible to maintain your financial safety net.

Insurance and Financial Security

Insurance is a financial arrangement or contract between an individual (or entity) and an insurance company. In exchange for regular premium payments, the insurance company agrees to provide financial protection or reimbursement against specific risks, losses, or liabilities. The purpose of insurance is to mitigate the financial impact of unforeseen events, allowing individuals or businesses to manage risks and safeguard their financial well-being.

Key Elements of Insurance

Premiums: Policyholders pay regular premiums (usually monthly or annually) to the insurance company.

Policy: The insurance policy is a legal contract outlining the terms, conditions, coverage, and exclusions of the insurance agreement.

Coverage: Insurance provides coverage for specified risks, such as health issues, accidents, property damage, or loss of life.

Claim: In the event of a covered loss or occurrence, the policyholder can file a claim to receive financial compensation or benefits from the insurance company.

Risk Pooling: Insurance operates on the principle of risk pooling, where numerous policyholders contribute premiums to create a fund that can be used to compensate those who experience covered losses.

Underwriting: Insurance companies assess risks before issuing policies, determining the likelihood of claims and setting appropriate premiums based on factors like age, health, or property value.

Insurance serves as a crucial tool in financial planning, offering protection against unexpected events and contributing to overall financial security and resilience.

Types of Insurance

Health Insurance: Protects against high medical costs.

Life Insurance: Provides financial security to dependents in the event of the policyholder's death. Property and Casualty Insurance: Covers damage to or loss of property and liability for injuries.

Assessing Coverage Needs: Evaluate your individual circumstances to determine the appropriate amount and types of insurance coverage needed.

Regular Review: Periodically review your insurance policies to ensure they align with your current life stage and financial situation.

Emergency Preparedness: While insurance provides a safety net, being prepared for emergencies through planning and risk mitigation strategies is equally important.

This chapter equips you with the tools to proactively manage unforeseen financial challenges. Building a robust emergency fund and understanding the role of insurance in your overall financial security plan lay the foundation for resilient and stable financial well-being.

CHAPTER 4

<u>INVESTING BASICS FOR BEGINNERS</u>

Investment refers to the act of allocating money, time, or resources with the expectation of generating future income, profit, or appreciation. In financial terms, an investment involves committing capital to an asset, venture, or project with the goal of obtaining a positive return on that investment over time.

Investing is the key to growing wealth over time. This chapter serves as your gateway to the world of investments, providing a foundational understanding and exploring low-risk options.

Introduction to Investments

- *Purpose of Investing:* Understand that investing is a means of making your money work for you, with the goal of generating returns and building wealth over time.

- *Risk and Reward:* Grasp the concept that higher returns often come with higher risks. It's crucial to align your investment strategy with your risk tolerance and financial goals.

- *Asset Classes:* Explore different asset classes, including stocks, bonds, and real estate, to diversify your investment portfolio.

- *Long-Term Perspective:* Investing is generally a long-term endeavor. Learn the power of compounding and the benefits of staying invested through market fluctuations.

Low-Risk Investment Options

Low-risk investment options are typically characterized by a lower probability of losing capital, making them more conservative choices. While these investments offer a higher level of security, they often come with lower potential returns compared to higher-risk alternatives. Here are some common low-risk investment options:

- Savings Accounts: While not high-yield, savings accounts offer liquidity and security for short-term goals and emergency funds.

- Certificates of Deposit (CDs): Low-risk, fixed-term investments that provide slightly higher interest rates than regular savings accounts.

- Government Bonds: Considered low-risk, as they are backed by the government. Bonds pay periodic interest and return the principal at maturity.

- Diversified Mutual Funds: These funds spread investments across various assets, reducing risk. They are managed by professionals, making them suitable for beginners.

- Annuities: Annuities are financial products that provide a stream of income for a specified period or for life. Fixed annuities offer guaranteed returns, making them a lower-risk option.

- Blue-Chip Stocks with Dividends: Investing in well-established companies with a history of stability and paying dividends can be a lower-risk equity option. While stocks inherently carry more risk than bonds, blue-chip stocks are generally considered less volatile.

- Money Market Funds: These funds invest in short-term, low-risk securities like Treasury bills and commercial paper. Money market funds aim to maintain a stable net asset value (NAV) and provide liquidity.

- Municipal Bonds: Issued by local governments, municipal bonds are considered relatively safe. They offer tax advantages for certain investors and provide regular interest payments

CHAPTER 5

TRACKING AND ADJUSTING YOUR BUDGET

Effective budgeting is an ongoing process. This chapter guides you through the importance of regular reviews and adapting your budget to life changes.

Regular Budget Reviews

A regular budget review is a systematic and periodic assessment of your financial plan and spending habits. It involves examining income, expenses, savings, and investments to ensure that your financial goals align with your current situation. Here's what a regular budget review typically entails:

- Frequency: Set a regular schedule for reviewing your budget, whether it's monthly, bi-monthly, or quarterly.

- Identifying Trends: Track your spending patterns over time to identify trends and areas for potential adjustments.

- Budget vs. Actual Comparison: Compare your planned budget with your actual spending. This helps you identify any deviations and understand their implications.

    1. Analyze the differences between your planned budget and your actual spending.

    2. Identify any trends or recurring patterns in your expenses.

3. Understand the reasons behind any significant variations.

- Celebrating Wins: Acknowledge and celebrate financial victories, whether it's reaching a savings goal or paying off a debt.

Adapting to Life Changes

Major Life Events: Adjust your budget to accommodate major life changes such as a new job, marriage, or the birth of a child.

Financial Goals Evolution: Your financial goals may evolve over time. Regularly assess and update them to align with your current priorities.

Emergency Fund Reassessment: After significant life changes, reassess the adequacy of your emergency fund to ensure it aligns with your new circumstances.

Professional Guidance: In times of substantial change, consider seeking advice from financial professionals to ensure your financial strategy remains sound.

Diving deep into investing and budgeting adjustments, these chapters empower you with the knowledge and tools to navigate the dynamic landscapes of wealth building and financial planning.

Building a Sustainable Financial Future

Long-Term Financial Planning

Set clear long-term financial goals, aligning them with your life aspirations.

Implement strategies for consistent wealth-building over time.

Understand the importance of adapting your plan as circumstances evolve.

Retirement Savings

Start saving for retirement early to benefit from the power of compounding.

Explore retirement investment vehicles such as 401(k)s and IRAs.

Regularly reassess and adjust your retirement savings strategy.

Pitfalls to Watch Out For

- Identify and avoid common pitfalls like underestimating expenses or neglecting an emergency fund.
- Be cautious of lifestyle inflation and impulsive spending habits.

Learning from Mistakes

Here are common budgeting mistakes to be aware of and learn from:

1. Not Having a Budget

Mistake: Failing to create a budget can lead to financial disorganization and overspending.

Lesson: Establishing a budget is foundational for effective financial management. It provides a roadmap for spending, saving, and achieving financial goals.

2. Underestimating Expenses

Mistake: Neglecting to account for all expenses can result in overspending and financial strain.

Lesson: Conduct a thorough analysis of both fixed and variable expenses. Include categories such as utilities, groceries, and and discretionary spending to ensure a comprehensive budget.

3. Ignoring Emergency Fund

Mistake: Neglecting to prioritize an emergency fund leaves you vulnerable to unexpected expenses.

Lesson: Allocate a portion of your budget to build and maintain an emergency fund. This financial safety net provides security during unforeseen circumstances.

4. Failing to Track Spending

Mistake: **No**t monitoring daily expenditures can lead to overspending and budget deviations.

Lesson: Regularly track and review your spending to identify patterns, adjust your budget as needed, and and maintain financial discipline.

5. Overlooking Debt Repayment

Mistake: Ignoring debt payments can lead to accumulating interest and financial stress.

Lesson: Prioritize debt repayment within your budget. Allocating funds to pay down debts helps reduce interest costs and improves overall financial health.

6. Setting Unrealistic Goals

Mistake: Establishing unattainable financial goals can lead to frustration and abandonment of budgeting efforts.

Lesson: Set realistic and achievable financial goals. Gradual progress is sustainable and contributes to long-term success.

7. Neglecting Adjustments for Life Changes

Mistake: Failing to adapt your budget to life changes, such as job loss or a salary increase, can result in financial imbalance.

Lesson: Regularly reassess and adjust your budget to align with changes in income, expenses, or financial goals.

8. Not Saving for Future Goals

Mistake: Forgetting to allocate funds for future goals like education, homeownership, or retirement can hinder long-term financial success.

*Lesson: I*ncorporate savings categories for specific future goals within your budget. Consistent contributions build a pathway to achieving these aspirations.

9. Ignoring Non-Monthly Expenses

Mistake: Neglecting irregular expenses, like annual insurance premiums or car maintenance, can lead to budget shortfalls.

Lesson: Anticipate and budget for non-monthly expenses by setting aside funds regularly. This prevents financial strain when these expenses arise.

10. Failing to Build a Buffer

Mistake: Operating without a buffer for unexpected expenses can disrupt your budget during challenging times.

Lesson: Include a miscellaneous or buffer category in your budget to accommodate unforeseen costs, providing flexibility and reducing financial stress.

Learning from these mistakes allows individuals to refine their budgeting approach, fostering financial discipline, and enhancing overall financial well-being.

- Embrace a mindset of continuous improvement in your budgeting practices.
- Analyze past mistakes to refine your approach and enhance financial resilience.

These chapters serve as a roadmap for building a sustainable financial future, emphasizing long-term planning, retirement savings, and the importance of learning from common budgeting pitfalls

CHAPTER 6

<u>SUCCESS STORIES AND TIPS FROM</u>

<u>BUDGETING PRO</u>

In this final chapter, we draw inspiration from real success stories and glean valuable tips from seasoned budgeting professionals. Learn from those who have mastered the art of budgeting and discover actionable strategies to elevate your financial journey.

<u>SUCCESS STORIES</u>

1. **Debt-Free Achievements:**

- Hear from individuals who successfully paid off significant debts using strategic budgeting and debt repayment plans.

2. Savings Milestones:

- Explore stories of individuals who transformed their financial lives by consistently saving and building robust emergency funds.

3. Investment Triumphs:

- Learn how savvy investors navigated the financial markets, growing their wealth through thoughtful investment sstrategies.

4. Financial Freedom Journeys:

- Dive into narratives of those who achieved financial independence by aligning their lifestyles with their values and diligently following budgeting principles.

TIPS FROM BUDGETING PROS

1. Set Clear Goals:

- Define specific, measurable, achievable, relevant, and time-bound (SMART) financial goals.

2. Prioritize Debt Repayment:

- Tackle high-interest debts first and employ debt snowball or debt avalanche methods for efficient repayment.

3. Emergency Fund First:

- Establish and prioritize an emergency fund as the foundation of your financial ssecurity.

4. Automate Savings:

- Use automated transfers to ensure consistent contributions to savings and investment accounts.

5. Budgeting Apps and Tools:

   - Leverage budgeting apps and tools for real-time tracking, visualization, and analysis of your finances.

6. Regularly Assess and Adjust:

   - Schedule regular budget reviews to assess progress and make necessary aadjustments.

7. Frugality with Purpose:

   - Embrace frugality not as deprivation but as a conscious choice aligned with your financial goals.

8. Diversify Investments:

- Consider diversifying your investments to manage risk and optimize returns.

9. Financial Education:

- Invest time in enhancing your financial literacy to make informed decisions and stay empowered.

10. Celebrate Milestones:

- Acknowledge and celebrate financial milestones, reinforcing positive financial habits.

These success stories and expert tips serve as a roadmap for your own budgeting journey. By learning from the experiences of others and

implementing proven strategies, you can achieve

financial success, build wealth, and enjoy a fulfilling

and secure financial future. Remember, your

financial journey is unique, and these insights are

tools to guide you toward your specific goals and

aspirations.

CONCLUSION

<u>NAVIGATING YOUR FINANCIAL JOURNEY</u>

As we conclude this guide, let's reflect on key takeaways and foster a mindset of continued financial growth.

Recap of Key Takeaways

- Budgeting Mastery: Budgeting is your financial compass, providing clarity and control.
- Emergency Preparedness: Build an emergency fund and secure your financial future through strategic insurance.

- Investing Insights: Understand the basics of investing and explore low-risk options for wealth building.

- Long-Term Vision: Plan for the future with long-term financial strategies and prudent retirement savings.

- Budgeting Wisdom: Learn from common mistakes, avoiding pitfalls and adapting your budget to life changes.

The Next Step to Financial Wellness

As we conclude this comprehensive guide, it's crucial to look beyond the pages of this book and consider the ongoing journey toward financial wellness. This chapter serves as a bridge between the knowledge gained and the proactive steps needed for sustained financial well-being.

Reflect on Your Financial Journey

Take a moment to reflect on the progress you've made through the budgeting, savings, investing, and financial planning insights shared in this guide. Acknowledge your achievements and areas for improvement.

Continuous Learning and Adaptation

Financial wellness is a dynamic concept that requires continuous learning and adaptation. Stay informed about changes in personal finance, investment strategies, and economic trends. Be open to adjusting your financial plan based on evolving circumstances.

Set Progressive Financial Goals:

Building on the goals outlined in your budget and savings strategies, set new, progressive financial goals. Whether it's increasing your emergency fund, diversifying your investments, or achieving a major life milestone, well-defined goals provide direction and motivation.

Explore Advanced Financial Strategies:

Consider exploring more advanced financial strategies as you gain confidence and experience. This may involve delving into tax planning, estate planning, or advanced investment strategies. Consulting with financial professionals can provide valuable insights tailored to your specific situation.

Leverage Technology and Tools

Take advantage of financial tools and technology to streamline your budgeting, track investments, and monitor your financial progress. Numerous apps and platforms are designed to enhance financial management and decision-making.

Seek Professional Guidance

If your financial situation becomes more complex or if you encounter challenges beyond your expertise, don't hesitate to seek professional guidance. Financial advisors, tax professionals, and legal experts can offer personalized advice aligned with your goals.

Build a Support System

Share your financial goals with trusted friends, family, or mentors. Building a support system can provide encouragement, accountability, and valuable perspectives as you navigate your financial journey.

Celebrate Financial Milestones

Celebrate your financial milestones, both big and small. Recognize the discipline and effort you've invested in achieving your goals. This positive reinforcement reinforces healthy financial habits.

This chapter serves as a call to action, urging you to embrace the ongoing process of financial wellness. By staying informed, setting progressive goals, exploring advanced strategies, leveraging technology, seeking guidance, building a support system, and celebrating achievements, you pave the way for a future of sustained financial well-being. Remember, your journey to financial wellness is a dynamic and empowering adventure. Keep moving forward with confidence and purpose.

Encouragement for Continued Financial Growth

Financial empowerment is a journey, not a destination. Keep embracing learning, adapt to life's twists, and celebrate your financial wins—no matter how small. Your commitment to building a sustainable financial future is the key to unlocking a life of security, opportunity, and fulfillment.

Thank you for joining this exploration of budgeting, savings, investing, and financial well-being. May your path to financial growth be rewarding and your journey toward a prosperous future be filled with success.